T0355942

SHADOW PRICE

SHADOW PRICE

POEMS

FARAH GHAFOOR

ANANSI

Published in Canada in 2025 and the USA in 2025 by House of Anansi Press Inc.
houseofanansi.com

29 28 27 26 25   1 2 3 4 5

Library and Archives Canada Cataloguing in Publication

Title: Shadow price : poems / Farah Ghafoor.
Names: Ghafoor, Farah, author.
Description: Includes bibliographical references.
Identifiers: Canadiana (print) 20240455282 | Canadiana (ebook) 20240460952 |
ISBN 9781487012922 (softcover) | ISBN 9781487012939 (EPUB)
Subjects: LCGFT: Poetry.
Classification: LCC PS8613.H344 S53 2025 | DDC C811/.6—dc23

Cover design: Alysia Shewchuk
Cover image: iStock.com/ilbusca
Book design and typesetting: Lucia Kim

House of Anansi Press is grateful for the privilege to work on and create from the Traditional Territory of many Nations, including the Anishinabeg, the Wendat, and the Haudenosaunee, as well as the Treaty Lands of the Mississaugas of the Credit.

Canada Council   Conseil des Arts
for the Arts   du Canada

ONTARIO ARTS COUNCIL
CONSEIL DES ARTS DE L'ONTARIO
an Ontario government agency
un organisme du gouvernement de l'Ontario

With the participation of the Government of Canada
Avec la participation du gouvernement du Canada | Canadä

We acknowledge for their financial support of our publishing program the Canada Council for the Arts, the Ontario Arts Council, and the Government of Canada.

Printed and bound in Canada

Contents

THE GARDEN

SHADOW PRICE

noun *(economics)*
the estimated price of a good or service for which no
market price exists

Shadow Price

Most people fault the industry instead of those greasing the gears. Risk averse and careful not to be specific. Without all of your information, the insurance company can only profit through group insurance. I almost worked in insurance. Whenever I'm in a car at a dangerous intersection, I think *If I die, I die.* There's only so much you can do away from the wheel. I take a class on healthcare economics and calculate the statistical value of a life. The more danger involved, the higher the wage to compensate. A market value that is inferred and not directly observed is called a shadow price. I take a class on the economics of education and complete my degree. I chose a safe major. I am risk averse, weak even. I am bad at lying, always ending with a laugh. What's so funny? We're all going to the same place anyway. I don't like to drive. I don't like the smell of oil. I imagine getting high off of it. I have never smoked anything. I'm risk averse, you see, and so, afraid of everything. Sometimes when a stranger speaks to me on public transportation, I jump. *The median estimate of a statistical value of a life is about $4.9 million.* I'm not tested on this, so I forget it. I'm looking for a job, preferably one that doesn't require driving. As a teenager, my hypothetical freedom was satiated from the safety of my bedroom. I read socialist articles on my phone as I was driven between orange cones, birds dropping dead outside the window. What a shame, I thought, fumes fluttering in my throat. I love birds. I imagined that they fell like stars and began typing out a poem. The past brims with dead things, cooling in the air conditioning. There must be a job to calculate their price. Demand is invented every day. The birds disappear under the heat and rain. They are buried by rocks, gravel, pavement. There is always construction going on, a kind of fossilization. Group insurance, balancing

out those who claim benefits and those who do not. You can argue that
the past doesn't exist. You can throw it into the drying river. You can set
it on fire, pour it into your car, get high off of it. I am an adult, so I am
predictable. I am an adult, so I drive. I choose to, or it is chosen for me.
Most economists do what they're told, you must understand. They quan-
tify the resources, calculate the risks, evaluate and present the numbers.
Often it is up to others to act on this information. Most people who want
to lead are following a higher order. Their futures are chosen for them
as they drive carefully through the construction, laughing *If I die, I die*,
learning to ignore even the child screaming next to them.

TIME

I have seen your true face: the back of your head.

Richard Siken

The Snail

You're going to die, I said
to the garden snails on the path as I rushed through the rain
toward the car, late as usual.

I stepped back for a moment, then, and knelt,
lifting by its shell into the grass the first snail,
like a millionaire selecting a child to sponsor.
The second, gracefully on route to the yard,
I left where it was.

When I returned from that dissatisfying lunch,
the sky the same threat of water, I remembered the second snail—
its nearly blind eyes raised like the heavy heads of flowers—
only to see in its place dark crushed petals.

That shell so small it could contain my life—
the shell that said, *You cannot continue
to live like this.*

The Dream-Eaters

Thousands of migrating birds have inexplicably died in south-western US in what ornithologists have described as a national tragedy that is likely to be related to the climate crisis.
    The Guardian

The tiny black moon of insect eclipsed
by the pad of my finger: there is nothing
more natural to me.

A little death of the least fit, soundless
as the violet fields of space
fenced by living stars.

My heart, soundless as a plague.

*

The stars abandoned by the sky, upon examination, are birds,
starved and breathless. They consumed the winds
beneath them and believed they would arrive at their destination,
inevitably trespassing.

In the photos, they lay in a line,
as if taken by a firing squad.
Our palms, under lotions,
are charred from the steel.

The fires of these lifetimes—
our violence could rival that foreign sun.

I write these words, and the poem ages
with me. What precedes translation
is the admission that language is the vestige
of all we did not say aloud.

✴

But what do I know of suffering?
This summer, we picked white blooms to last a week
in our crystal vases. Their siblings flourished safely
into berries and figs, wild as dusk.

We feasted, calling them gifts.
Even the earth is a present
if we echo it loudly enough.
Even time can serve you—

decorated in fruit and forest is, after all,
the first museum of looted treasure.

Inside our mouth lay the artist,
the wasp, which, too, was eaten
by its masterpiece.

✴

For years, I blamed only the terrible moods
of the world. Now I drag a rag harder
over the blot on my reflection.

The child in me watches the news on loop.
In each desire, a negotiation
with the old woman beside her.

At the end of the show,
flowering from between the predator's teeth
is a spine, a matted mane,
a sudden face.

✳

For mirrors, we excavate the rivers for sand.
For moguls, we hack glaciers into cocktail cubes.
For more, we import ease, return our waste overseas.

There is a solution for every dream,
explain the dream-eaters. *Don't be afraid
of success.*

A ray of light wakes the telescope.
We measure the sunset down
to the degree, time to the millisecond.

In fight-flight-or-freeze, the heart speaks
back to you: *Focus—*
you're still here.

An iceberg, unmoving and sharp,
is aimed at our lens.

*

It's the third decade of the twentieth century
and your grandmother has your eyes.
It's the third decade of the twenty-first century
and you have your granddaughter's eyes.

A hand pushes your hair behind your ear.
Rilke said that nearby is the country
they call life,

so keep the light on
when we leave.

Bigfoot, Mayor of Carbonland

When our mountains were pervaded with smoke, we slept
through its black commotion, masked as directed,
until the sky cleared to a healthy copper. Its glow reflected
onto the lakes coated in aluminum wire, oil, and the glimmering
plastic wrap that Bigfoot had given us out of the goodness

of his heart. That heart, invisible and rich
as a rumour, was so romantic he asked for everyone's hand
in marriage. Florid as the air and the water, we submitted
to his ember gaze, before that handsome suit. We let
our better half name the children and schedule in their lives
proper schooling and work shifts at Bigfoot Industries.

When the children overnight were hewn like redwood
by the smoke's thick arms, his press release suggested we change
our ovens. So we built more efficient ones with Bigfoot materials,
and were commissioned by Bigfoot to promote them with our best recipes,
the most luxurious fruits of which we offered to him.

When the children, off work and playing ball in the streets,
were stampeded by the fat hooves of his red cows,
Bigfoot's newspaper suggested meatless Mondays
and gardening, after which from the windows the cows
stared into our faithfully fresh salads with their myriad digital eyes.

When the children, eyes dried to sand by the teething heat,
crashed their Bigfoot cars, his engineers kindly installed
extra mirrors, and his representatives thoughtfully lobbied
for more effectual driving lessons, which the children took before passing
away in his hospitals, their bodies hidden from public view.

When the fish ingested all of the Bigfoot water bottles,
sheet masks, and other daily items in the lakes
and entered sterile into our beautiful new era, we pitied them
over funeral dinners of supple Bigfoot seafood.
Eyeless and boneless, they were convenient sources
of energy, especially for the underprivileged, to gorge on
and for which we thanked Bigfoot at every meal.

When some of us, between distractions, missed our children
and put forward a complaint, Bigfoot invited us
to an official presentation in the square of his downtown office.
Shot through our uniformed security dogs and projected
onto every screen in the city, he stood tall as a flag
and anthemed a white shining welcome.

With his long tongue he sweetly gifted us
constructive feedback on how in the mirrored rooms
of our houses we could fix
ourselves, and we accepted it all with appropriate concern
and pleasure as our children's children
were sold to the market behind our bolted chairs.

And as always, when Bigfoot strode silently away
to tend to the media, he left a hot shimmer
of perfume above footprints as wide and deep as canyons.
Out of politeness, we never questioned them, not even then,
returning quietly to our underground Bigfoot homes,
which were as dark and wooden and predictable as the night.

Devotion

JULY 20█ SIBERIA

A mammoth graveyard is discovered in permafrost, which, when
thawed, will release carbon dioxide and methane as well as unknown
diseases.

Of course it was 326 bones you and I began with,
scattered in Russian permafrost: four mammoth feet,
four wisdom teeth, one scalloped jaw unlatched,
yards and yards of galactic shards unaware
that one day they would be, by two hands, borne
into the glaring light of the future—

A prognosis I couldn't have fended off
with two opal swords, but I had no will, anyways,
in our icy womb. Generous and furred
as love, our shared blood met at some strange apex
in the wild white rooms of history,
where your footsteps caverned over
the dozen tiny moons of my first crawl.

Beneath the snow, the past is still wakeful
as a harp, its horizontal hunt perforated with spears
as blinding and prescient as stars.
From this polar bed, then,

we emerge, diseased and mystic,
into a world once our own.

Like a foreign salve, a magnetic blade,
a silver trophy to raise above one's head.

As my predecessors ordained, you and I
will sweeten the air irreversibly, making sicknesses
of the years they have casted us into.
In anticipation, I have split this crooked rib
to keep each half of us company—

The crescent beacon preluding ash, warm as the mouth
of the excavator on the brim of our skull.
A mercurial drink, a stellar dust, any desire
to live eclipsed by his fist as he exhibits us
before a sparkling audience,
weeping.

Tomorrow

There is still time, so approve the project. Comply with the law, or don't. It's not the end of the world. Find a way to minimize expenses. Cut those jobs, they'll be fine. The future is a tightrope. Lengthen it with cash. Lengthen it with flights overseas, the air is clear enough. The pilot will be fine. The kids will be fine. Look them in the eye. Try again. That's it. Smile. Collect donations from customers. Tell them they are right, that they are, in fact, tax-deductible. Tell the customer they have rights, then hire a private army. Where can they run? They'll be fine if they don't breach any policies, remember that they're on camera, and keep their receipts ready for review. If they spend less on coffee, generate another stream of passive income, and buy headphones that will change their life. They'll be fine with a musical view of their lawns. Certain the neighbours of the houses they will one day own will be fine. Loan them wood and tools and rope anyway with a payment plan and the lowest interest around. Offer them a response personalized with their name, birthday, and social insurance number. Say: *It's going to be okay, okay? It will be okay, so close your eyes.* Everything will be fine. Tuck them in and shut off the lights. Good night, sweet dreams, we will see you tomorrow.

Natural History Museum

The Present visits once a year, always on an arbitrary date.
It visits with children to see newness circulated through the houses
of the past. The Present looks around, buys a postcard
or an accessory from the gift shop to place at the bottom of a drawer,
then leaves behind the skeletons of its former selves.
Their bones are still and white as distant planets, smoothed and sharpened
into points. The Present is reminded of its bones only when broken,
and then the Future is considered, its supposed desires
and plans. The Future, for whom the door is always open,
a sweet wind blowing in petals and leaves, sticks and feathers.
The same doorway through which the Present passes,
and forgets what it was doing, its reasons why.
Then, the Present is awoken by birds, who are made
of the Past. Naturally, they are named, fed well,
caged, stuffed, and donated to the museum. One of them
the Present takes home and mounts on the wall
like a white lie under which the Future will be spoken of
with possessives. To the museum, the Future remains
a legendary knight, a spectral mentor, a mysterious lover
who never arrives, never touches anything in the shelters
of the Present or the Past. The museum is subject
to the eyes of the visitor, of course, and bends like light
under its laws, mirrors, offspring. The air inside
is tightened like a fist over the throats of the exhibits.
In the blur, you can almost see someone coming.

The Subject

When I saw the Empire, I was impressed
by its facade. The marble maps gleamed as if untouched,
stone statues simmering pale in the heat.
How beautiful the cathedral sheltering the tomb
of the explorer, its architecture now imitated
atop office buildings on purloined shores.
Up the mountains were orchards of olives and dates,
pigs and cows smouldering in the shade, and, stagnant
as water, the people of the supposed future.
Across the land, the bleached white walls of courtyards
continued into castles and into the rings.
I saw the ghosts of bulls everywhere,
breeds born to die on Sundays.
What else is there to say? I paid money to see
my place in the world, spent my life to view
my blood on every glittering surface.
In the evenings, my hands were empty,
so to eat and drink, I was penalized with nouns.
At the museum, the paintings of costumed men were immaculate.
The shading so soft, the light in their eyes so difficult to discern
that they followed you. Everywhere, my back
was probed with steel, and stare, and strange shadow.
In the harsh light, I darkened.
The hours scabbed over each other.
I looked hard at the time, my feet dusty and sore.
Come here, they said. *This is tradition.*

The inquisition lasted for only hundreds of years.
I had known only air conditioning, a distant weeping
like waves across the earth. A textbook, a news article
read on my cellphone, a plane ticket in the opposite hand.
But subject has always been a verb,
and every face of language a flag.
The past is a profitable industry,
a destination that will educate you on its edges.
I know what I am to them now.
I have seen my destined nose ring,
my invisible horns curling up toward the heavens.

The Jungle Book: Epilogue

I.

I've been lying for a long time, so let me tell you a story.
Despite the bravado of the dog quaking before the wolf,
we can never go back to who we were. Despite the dream
to be left alone, untouched. Where flesh rustles
like a fire, begging on four legs, for meat, any kind
of meat, shaking the thought from its skull, a skull
hollow as the sly wolf's slyer moon. Its hidden face
whispers into the flaring ear of the sun, who
considers our potential in the mechanics of space.
The world fogs, warily, in our defence,

but the damage has been done, and so returned
and reintroduced is the dream to the land.
Plant a body in the forest and wait for an arc, a plot,
a villain. One twist after another until the light ends. Physics
or God, it depends now on who is telling the story.
The wolf knows what you've inherited so call both the wolf
and the moon monsters. No one will stop you.

II.

The story of the boy in the forest ends with the death
of the forest's king. A boy found in the dirt will win
when there's nothing to be won. The king's hunger
merely another river. Survival as a result of killing
begets a future of killing incomplete without the ally,
friend, father. So at the boy's side is the bear. The boy
would be dead without the bear, and the bear, who eats
uncomplaining insects and fruit, is harmless without the boy.
You must make a decision: the boy or the bear. The king
is dead and only one can be left alone. So place them
in a cage of heat and wait for an impossible past
to resurface, to touch this new world. The boy's mother,
a figment of sky and earth, is dead, so he has nothing
to lose. The bear has its body, a proxy. This could take
a while, but if the boy is a liar, he will kill the insects
and eat the fruit. If not, this will end quickly.
They have all the time in the world,
but the story must end, as all stories do.

III.

Seize the forest and build the new world from its flesh.
Out of the smoke a figure emerges and sits on a throne warmed
by bones. *Blood for blood*, parrots the dog. For scraps it whines,
wags, never recalls the wolf until both are thrown into a stadium,
a fire, a prophecy, a dream. The victor will eat next to
the throne while the sun's eyes are elsewhere and the moon
dances for us. The pendulum moves in both directions,
despite gravity, in spite of fate, gleaming gold and red
as the horizon. Tell me, what is there left to become?
An arrow with a rope tied to the end, splitting the smoke
to pierce the sun? Or the stone carving the moon's pearl jaw?
There is no truth. There are only these hands,
and even they are sharpened by your gaze. Even they,
here in the dark, will mistake memory and myth.

The Colony

It's true, there are millions of us on this collapsing
mound of dirt. Let's not think about the queen. Each day
is an opportunity to bring home beauty in the shape
of a leaf, a moth, a seed. Together we eat,
we burn, and like air, we float when the earth floods.

Some are forced into the water first, their names redacted
from our language, but we never forget their faces,
those fierce barbed mouths and shining skin.
In another life, we were soft, but our flesh has turned
inside out to weather a past we cannot see.

Let's not think about the queen on our backs,
her resolutions heavy with honey and milk,
her image refracting into a thousand expressions.
The dream of her is the weight of the sky

so don't look up. Take my hand, link
your arm through mine, and hold your breath.
We will make a boat of our bodies,
swim up and out into the light.

We will reach the end
of the river in hours, in years,
and the home we claim for ourselves
will be the land under our feet.

Evolution

In the land of the dead, contentment   is another's mourning

      The bursting dawns   of gazelle, zebra, wildebeest

are born ready to run   readier to die wading

      through the prongs   of the savannah's flammable

crown. Lying in my dirt bed   I brand the herds

      Myopia, Denial, Uncertainty   *Destiny*

and knight them by whatever names   they desire.

      I don't care where a word comes from,

only what it will do   to me, so I capitalize

      my black-maned haunt   *Prince, Necropolitics,*

Economy of Misfortune. Under this syntax

      of sunlight, I surveil   for epiphany, shadow

like a frustrated door   of clouds.

      Dear Honeyblooded,   won't you tune for me

an ambered fate, a dance atop beauty

until your soles split like embers?

Despair for me   a song, so I can pluck

the streaming fiddle   of your long Godwatered throat?

Dear vacillating meadows of opportunity   equip my silence

Chittering wild-dog heart   pay your dues, pay

attention   Thieving hyena mouth   supply now to demand

tomorrow, or else humiliate   the walk home

Tomorrow   will arrest us anyway   back to the earth

and disinherit our most vain tools. So take

and outlast necessity   Today is a digression

a feast, a war chariot   on fire

The sky burns   like an arrow   but my eyes are gilt dare

My body is the decree   the synapse   the endless gale:

the terrible stride   of a blade that knows exactly   what is coming—

The Whale

*We live in capitalism, its power seems inescapable—but then, so did
the divine right of kings.*
  Ursula K. Le Guin

The whale is worth over two million dollars
as an international public good. What am I worth, I'm asked,
until I start investing? If I want to make it, that is—make it
to a table of portfolios diverse in national economies,
with an account I call by a Swiss pet name,
new enough to "put the fun in funds."

Between the clouds in a room made of one-way glass,
I too would call for order, clicking incessantly the button
atop my designer scepter, held high above my hairless, glimmering crown,
when the residents below do not compete politely for the coins
tossed generously into the air. The copper lands on the royal hunting grounds,
on subsidized, corporate properties, and between foreign, democratized wells.
Sometimes, it lands in disputed territories. Sometimes, in the sea.
The residents are commanded to remain still, hands behind their head,
otherwise they will be stunted productively by all authorities.
This I would decree via pamphlets released on the wind,
signing special editions on holidays, and publishing them
with other rulings in a slim folder that the residents may keep
beside their embossed books in hotel nightstands.

I am the future, I'm told, so invest now
to live like this, to say I've made it. I am made

of carbon in all dimensions of time, in my business-formal attire,
in an unconscious state tilled through the days
the way a whale is dragged forward by the current. It cycles carbon
through its lungs, amassing value—efficient production
appraised at millions of dollars if you consider its impact
on industrial fishing and ecotourism. Big money

moving into a big mouth, sliding over a big tongue into a belly
big enough to sleep inside. Here, in the whale,
I've just woken up. I light a lamp and cup my faith over it
until it's no longer numb, yellow blubber whispering at the cusp.
This room is rented and flooding, but location, as they say,
is everything, and here the air tastes as clean as it is not.
I ask around, and find out this is a new-hire orientation.
Wonderful! I think, then turn around and learn

that it is a funeral reception. *Oh no*, I say.
Who died? I ask my friends and family, my neighbours
and coworkers, the CEO and receptionist,
recruiters, writers, brand strategists, journalists,
lawyers, lobbyists, landlords, developers, podcasters,
publicists, auditors, academics, diplomats, bureaucrats,
consultants, phone scammers, celebrities, influencers,
artificial intelligence and all of its dogs
but everyone is speaking over each other.
I press my ear to each conversation, turn it like a safe lock,
but never hear my persuasion click. My bait was never precise
enough for networking, but I'm not too dissatisfied—

I have plenty of work left to complete. I just bought
an ergonomic chair to mitigate the risk of my feet
liquifying into the slippery floor of the whale's stomach lining.
My body will thank me for it, I'm told, by labouring
at least five to ten years past expiration. *Thank you for making it,*
a modulated voice announces over the heads of the crowd.
Today's fun fact: researchers have discovered
that humans can live up to one hundred and fifty years.
In celebration, the booming bass accelerates
and attendees begin to bob frantically, panting, some stumbling
into other organs. I myself am nearly knocked out
of my seat and clutch a stranger's arm for balance.
One trillion dollars, he whispers, *was the value of whale stock*
six years ago, so imagine what it might be now. I should reconsider
liquidating my stock compensation, the business mogul advises further,
yanking his furred coat cuff out of my hand. Apparently, the residents
of the whale sector are not sufficiently motivated
to pay their breathing subscription. The cost
of living is rising like hot air, I realize,

as I am shot out through the whale's blowhole.
Briefly, I'm suspended in unfamiliar warmth.
My chest splits green as a seed and I open my eyes to a land
I swear I've seen—perhaps in childhood, perhaps
in a dream. There are creatures who look at me
without fear. Titans dressed in leaves even wave to me
like an old friend. I raise my hand,

then plunge back into the dark of the whale's body.
Disoriented, attention centres me, so I begin to gossip
about news that gusted through me moments before:
the whale's cousins are rebelling against local political forces
and the fish cannot marry because the scent of home
has been burnt from the water. *That behaviour
is so unprofitable!* someone exclaims. *It gets worse*, I continue,
*Words have blanched entire civilizations from the reef,
so rumours tend to float among ghosts until they too dissolve.*

Like my ears, which are melting off my skull, so I announce
that unfortunately, we will have to circle back on this, folks.
The crowd thins while I hold the two fleshy wings up by the lobes,
my many piercings still glinting, and think I may finally

be finding peace. A comfortable lifestyle
of self-help manuals, supplements, hot yoga, and meditation
until my brain steams, ready to present on a delicate platter.
I've built an audience to share what I've learned
on my journey, and monologue about how, previously, I had always eaten
what I was given, licked my plate until it shined
like a mythical moon, though that image too is an approximation.
Won't you invest in me? I call out, pointing
at each round, silvery face, and the cave echoes back,
ceiling dripping gastric acid a little faster than before.
I was taught that my disintegrating body
could be moulded into a glowing, manicured hand,

however, the echo fished out from my throat
my voice. The value that clung to my hems
like a shadow now places on me a target
for corporate solutions to bid on.
The value, contorting its lips, tells me that, unfortunately,
the role of my lungs has been made redundant, and my heart
dismissed. To obtain my severance package, I will be required
to hold my breath until further notice.
Of course, I can barely register all of this
without the aural support that my insurance did not cover.
Mulling over this update, I return to my room in the whale's esophagus
and find it has been sublet to tenants more compliant than I am.
In search of a place to sleep, then, I slide up and away

until I tumble into the whale's voicebox.
Cold and wiped clean, it has not sung in a while,
and I've lost track of its age, so I stand,
and luckily find myself swaying to its swimming rhythm.
It's still kicking! Thank God. A light spills onto the floor
behind me, filling the outline where my shadow once decomposed.
I look up, and what I believe to be the moon
is dangling its long arms through the blowhole, beckoning.
All this time, I thought it had been a spotlight.
I gasp as pain names each muscle, organ. It pauses
in my stomach, and I see that soon only my hands
will be left intact. What can they possibly do now?
This room is clogged with spirits who have danced
their flesh away, and the volume of this melody
is boring through my skin. The songs of the outside

had, for seconds, balmed my raw feet, softened
my shoulders. The language was strange
but the lilt of it, I realize now, matched the voice
in the back of my head. The one I had disposed of
to live happily in this world.

The moon still watching, its gaze intimate
as a fossil, I think that perhaps I want to hear
that fascinating tune once more. I bury my face
in my palms in supplication, breathe,
then reach up as high as I can.

Birthday Poem

The year I was born, we defined climate change denial.
It was the perfect name: three little words
to fit inside a sob.

Like my face, the future didn't exist yet,
but I felt its itch.

I felt its hand
over my erupting mouth.

✳

The neighbourhood standing on the dime
lake and the sign warning Thin Ice,
the bird silent

below the window. We saw it
coming, the fields vacant
of grasses and fauna.

Cardinal gash across the glass.
A century ago, it would have been a tagged passenger pigeon
and I would pick some discourse from its loosened beak.

Today, I forget its name in conversation
with my wretched hands
as they try to lift the window from its coma.

Through that silver-blue
we saw it coming
from miles away.

*

On top of the world, we skate.
Ice breaks like an apology
and you press harder on its sweating throat.

This is a joke—nothing can be made
human.

The ice shows you
only your face.

*

I found spring in January, October
clinging to my sandals, and said
nothing to the back of your head.

Your brain drenched in oil,
spine wrapped with feathers,
and fashionably shrouded in plastic—

Comical, isn't it?
That indestructible white
feigning the sky's honesty.

*

The hand edits, and the tortoise runs
into the clearing. I watch you affix fresh teeth
to the season. You say you'll give me

better hands in the clearing:
long, sharp nails and fingers
accessorized in gold and ivory.

Like any beast, I'll evolve—
dragged by my white pixelated outline—
into a curated vision.

In the distance, a crowd moves
like a fire.

The screen goes black,
starless.

*

Into my skull I empty
artificial rain: ten hours of it
once belonging to some other girl,
some other year.

Lie awake, lay asleep:
eyes closed, minds whirring
with fantasy. Of course

I'm having a good time.
I understand what this means.
I've seen this dream too:

the city we've built together,
your palms burnt with blood.

In the end, you snapped my neck
to look up at this future
we've made.

You held my hand.

*

I've seen your death in the weather, in your car,
in the package on your doorstep.

Graceful, at the centre
of your life.

What are you so afraid of?
You bought it.

You bought it for me.
You bought it for us, for me,
for my birthday.

I'm ███████ years old,
didn't you know?

I'm ███████ years old
and I'm going to die
with all of you.

THE LAST POET IN THE WORLD

The Last Poet in the World

Upon realizing it was uninvited, the moon escapes
the New Year's celebrations and rolls into the ocean.
The rainforest quietly unweaves its chemical shrines,
denying further aid, and the homing pigeons,
accused of treason, are promptly eliminated.
The immortal jellyfish, however, persist, bloodless
and brainless, on hunger, and natural selection resumes.
Artificial light reproduces with plastic, privately bred
by approximately ten percent of men, women, and children.
Such figures have an address, so naturally, evil must be
a neighbourhood on a space shuttle. And from the sky,
hundreds of thousands of lightning bolts touch down on the ground

and ring the doorbell. I open the door and discover
no one, and so here I am, back where I started.
Without superpower. Without beauty. Without
fins or wings, I inch along the marble floors
where I once knelt, thinking this is not
the end of the world but it could be,
as I licked a king's fingers, his scythe. Its edge
I held to my throat like a crown, a crescent, a collar

I would wear on Noah's Ark. After all, it was on a floodplain
that this city was built. Everyone says it's the perfect place to retire,
to die. Protestors will step off the streets in their wet shoes,

the presses will hoist their manifestos up to dry
in the wind, the politicians will fly back to their islands
in the meantime, and I—

I will not be buried but shipped
to the last museum and exhibited underneath my lifetime
achievement award, adorned in my soundless name,
with not even the moon there to object.

Very early in my life it was too late.

Marguerite Duras

.

As a child I was told that what is given can also be taken away.
Like the moon drawing back the tides before the turtles' sandy shells,
worms in the blue rain under the clouds' whims.
About the future, they say, don't worry. One night bound
to the next with labour.
I had always frowned, then looked around and saw
nobody else staring at the sun.
In their tinted glasses and expensive creams
while I squirmed at their feet.

For the Greeks, an apocalypse meant a revelation.
For days, I mine away at a sentence
while the world sheds its skin, tail in its puckered mouth.
For sleep, I wear a silk mask over my eyes.

There is beauty in everything, says the poem, so go find it.
If you tilt the mirror, there is an angle
that reveals what is not intended to be seen.
It can make a life seem bigger,
interior decorators will tell you.
Perhaps the mirror is the most unnatural invention—
water will distort but never lie.
You can appraise an object, label it, put it on display

but if you turned around, what would disappear?
My peers would have disagreed but the mirror explains
that maybe if, for once, we shut our eyes,
everything, everything will be beautiful
whether you want it to be or not.

I found a British man who drives out to the water every weekend.

A mallet in each hand, he treads over the flat black rock shining with the cold.

He kicks over stones, halts, then continues further into time.

I watch the back of his head categorize this indiscernible market.

When his rubber boot approves, he arcs his weapon toward the earth.

The white sky wakens and out yolks a fossil, a fossil to sell.

He lifts it to his mouth and I think, This must be a dream.

A dream, but when he turns around, then,

I see nothing but my own face.

There is a story in which I am innocent.
Everything is done to me just as the river is done to the rock around it.
A cool touch of blue at my neck, heat kneading my face.
There are dried roses, lilies, and carnations
in a glass jar near my desk.
I couldn't keep them alive.

No, that's not right.

Each night I returned home to see a shadow disfigure the water
then allocated my gaze to the window where the city moved on its own.
After I sought to save the fragile heads, I was surprised—
scent bears time from their bodies even inside a trashcan.

They still call the place where I was raised the city of roses,
though the remaining buds are cultivated artificially into the future.
There, the sun lands in the red palm of the horizon,
waiting, supposedly, for the perfect moment to explode.

Maybe I should've been a stenographer. Maybe their pen. Maybe converting passersby on the street with a microphone in the hollows of winter. Maybe the rat in the subway, the ant chewing on a green leak in the sidewalk. Maybe the leaf and its painless days. The first tree cut down for its concrete twin, screaming. How the air would remember the echoes, would be warped by them, like ice, like fire—What if it shimmered instead. No need for speech any longer, for words to be compiled until they amass meaning, until green means *go* and red *stop*, until poetry. What is poetry at the intersection. The cars crash regardless. The pedestrian always in danger. There will always be someone waiting at the corner. I'm at the corner now, rerouting, rerouting, my life at the centre of the intersection, reading a poem. I should have been a bird flying above it all. A gust of wind with no eyes, no mind, just a long desire to destination. Or a cloud sleeping and micturating in routine. Letting water pass through me like a gesture, a sound. I would pour over the earth, not knowing if I'm living or dying, or if this, like all passages, is the one destined for me.

It's been raining all January. The earth slows like a top urged on by a child whose father let him win the races, whose mother praised him for his appetite. As a child I stared like a clock through the window. The economy shuttered open and closed until my classmates gave up on working for NASA. I skip the tour of the rockets and lie in the hotel bed instead. Spring is in the air, fat and squawking with nothing to lose. The brave frogs doze in their puddles, their eyes glimmering coins. Beside the worms and snails, I take painkillers for the beloved weather that now boils my head to steam. I watch the delicate white sky take first my hands, then my face. Somewhere, a kettle is losing its voice.

It was so warm last night the mosquitoes slipped underneath my sleeves and bit me after years of elusion. I marvelled at the pear shape swelling like a memory on my skin, and the fireflies hovered, curious as stars. But I suppose that's not what really happened.

I'm home for the weekend, wading through the blossoms of July. I take the same walk through the neighbourhood and sit in the same back garden, naming dragonflies and beetles. I can't resist reading in this weather, as if absorption does one any good, as if I was the sea and the forest, taking air until breakage. It's easy to rest your eyes on the shivering leaves. Greenery here cocoons you until you wake, and you see its bars of teeth.

Once while driving I caught the thrashing sun in the rearview. I felt its breath in my chest, knowing that in a few streets I'd be able to pull into the driveway, but by then it had disappeared under a violet wave. Another afternoon, a rainbow appeared and I swerved, nearly crashing. How suburban, I thought, and remembered that rainbows emerge as glinting rings. The silent arch of light stood there, waiting for a metaphor, until I returned to my life.

Across the black pond, young geese were led safely as the sky boomed above, crackled behind me. I didn't turn around when the shouting persisted, some kind of light tearing itself apart inside the dark. Punishment, I imagine.

In my hands, this poem is turning clean,

and tidy, and safe,
making me

making me afraid.

The critic sighs their minutes into hours and the writer wails so the editor takes down the review as the river clasps around their ankles and night crushes even the ants back into the earth and wind pesters the windows for an encore and the children are turned in their beds like good dough and the naked deciduous, finally alone, pity the human language and the stars imagine a life of decision and the moon performs its small vanities and the sedentary flocks do not think about the moon at all and the clouds hold their breath until they crumble and the crumpled mountains ache for their native rock and the machines stare with their long eyes into the enduring dark and the iceberg floats into a dreamless coma and the stories all begin and end on the same note of music.

Reading comics and eating ice cream, despite bodily protests. *Do I need to feel anything?* I asked the ceiling before bed each night. I commuted to work and back, wore flattering expressions. The eggplant rotted, as did the tomatoes and bell peppers, and I seethed. Nothing happened to me, other than the slight ballooning. It was warm, then cold. The trees outside performed their flashy dying rituals, and I observed dutifully, then turned away. The sun, too, fizzled, and shadows stumbled down my face. My coughs paraded from my throat to announce my life, and my life appeared like bright white insects across my vision. They crawled away from the poems spectating in the cobwebs of the world.

Everyone assumed they would live for a long time
as our fevers broke like heat records, the sea snuck past
to the next house, and money ate through our varnished lives
like termites until the ceilings and walls collapsed onto our TV dinners.
Neighbourhoods, cities, nations were overcome by these invisible invasions.
Those who protested were soon replaced by silences.
A man lit himself on fire in front of the theatre of justice
and his ashes were promptly swept away while the newscasters
worried about the price of gas terrorizing the masses.
We returned to work and to classes, to the cafes and the bars,
to the gyms and the malls and the games, and then
to our varying screens. The glow perforated our face serums
to enter our bloodstreams until we became digital gods,
sleeping and waking to six-second videos.
I, too, wanted the praise and hearts of followers.
I, too, dreamed about my name beside a series of digits,
on a large screen in a public space, above crowds
waving their arms and screaming with indecipherable emotion.

Why have a life

when you can have a sentence
and a willing hand.

With precision you can create time,
call it indoors with its soaked fur and disinterested gaze
and kill it, too.

And with determination
an end arrives, pleading,
its face a brutal stone.

THE PLOT

There are trees breathing over one hundred years after decapitation. Stumps, dead to most passing eyes, fed by neighbouring trees through root grafts, soil pores, or fungi. The science on this subject is convoluted, which means anyone can narrate.

There is a story in which you surrendered, in which you guided the blade to your neck. The just, civilized blade with the will to build a greater world. The soldiers looted your limbs, your viridescent crown, your home.

Then, all at once, your mind is sheared flat and smooth as a stone. A gyre thumbed open for the sky, the past swirling into the future.

Your memory is to be crushed, bleached, refined, beaten, and pressed into paper upon which your history will be smothered by the oppressor's account, their image.

The right to live. The right to the land in which your roots travel eight feet into three pliant dimensions.

Siken: A tool in a certain hand is renamed a weapon. Such as evidence, such as testimony tremulous as water.

Without a witness, can a tree make a sound?

A man in Georgia loved a white oak in his childhood, thus it gained the right to own itself. The deed too exists only in the mouths of ghosts, so the law dissolves under the tongue of the public.

A natural person is born into their personhood; however, the tree, having seen hundreds of years, was rewarded for its memorability with legal personhood. Under the caress of the locals, its deeds will never involve revolt, inconvenience, desire.

An ideal subject will showcase the generosity of its owners, the state.

Natural trees read the names carved into their skin, the lips skimming their leaves for a bite. Warn their neighbours, hushed underground or fuming above, and call out for help. They remember what they've learned.

Land a tree in the city street, in the designated square between buildings, and it will likely bear the insects and diseases on its own.

In the fields slashed into neat rows, plants are bred out of their ability to speak. Corpses doused in chemical, they behold the swarms until the end.

A plot, thus a cast. A story, thus an antagonist.

(Though the pest, too, was born with a mouth, an expected lifespan. Without natural personhood.)

If there is conflict, there is a way to win. A tool to enter the bodies of the locals. The native cankerworms, with a hunger for anything from hardwoods to fruit trees, have maimed forests that always scabbed over their wounds in private.

Whereas codling moths and apple aphids nestled in imports two hundred years ago. In a story of trade, the economy, rules and regulations.

The histories, too, of waterway damage, induced famine, disease dissemination via supplies and larvae as strategy. Birth defects, links to movement and memory loss, and death for the consumers—winged or not.

Antagonist to orchards, to plantation forests where timber is reaped. The weather spoiling like a naive fruit. Clouds of insects are replaced by clouds of chemical, seeded artificially or not.

A matter of property, so a matter of law. A matter of home, so a matter of survival. A matter of power, so the glue trap, the slow poison, the wall of bricks and cement.

Antagonist to a dream, a vision. To production in which a hand runs the fountains, steadies the hose.

Herbicides, too, are used by loggers to melt down the competition in natural forests for abundant pulp and paper.

In the domesticated wildernesses eagerly sought by so many settlers, including me.

I know what you're thinking.

This trail of thought would unravel a life.

One hundred years old is young for a tree, when parents live for millenia, when grandparents are believed to be immortal.

The average lifespan on a timber plantation varies between thirty and eighty years. Selected for their species and age, then evenly situated and managed by human hands. Optimized for economic goods and services. The ability to produce without causing any real, extensive trauma to most consumers.

The purpose of these plantations is to protect the natural forests from us, we who establish ourselves in the land.

First, you must claim the land as yours, then clear it of its original inhabitants. Split their roots so they cannot depend on one another, then ready a chopping block.

Forest plantations are an essential tool of modern forest management, which in turn is an effort to regulate human activity, to ensure the sustainability of resources.

For some, the story begins here. On paper, we have protagonists. In print, a definition of sustainability first appeared in a book in 1713 after centuries of resource depletion in Europe. An emphasis on economic continuity, environmental balance, and social ethics led to the design of the first tree plantation for German timber production by the end of the eighteenth century.

Carlowitz, the son of the royal forester and a high-ranking finance manager for the Saxon mining sector, is considered the father of sustainability. His work provided a tract for Georg Ludwig Hartig and Heinrich Cotta, the fathers of modern forestry, who in turn produced the success of Sir Dietrich Brandis, the father of tropical forestry.

Narrative, according to Aristotle, requires three events: equilibrium—disruption—equilibrium, or balance—imbalance—balance.

The scene has been set and the characters introduced, granted the power to think on our behalf.

With wide eyes, we await catharsis.

The teak forests of India and Burma were subject to ruthless exploitation throughout the nineteenth century under British rule. Though timber plantations were initiated alongside clearcutting for tea, cinchona, and coffee cultivation, only the two growing teak and exotic eucalyptus were prosperous. So, in the name of conservation, the state further tightened its fist over indigenous forests in 1865 via monopoly.

The Department of Forestry, led by Brandis, jailed the indigenous forest dwellers who used arson to protest their stolen rights and the access upon which their lives were entirely dependent.

Since 2006, only three percent have had their rights and access returned through claims, though many reserves have evicted and displaced the same communities in a now permanently disfigured landscape.

Magnaeson: The effects of global events such as climate change can be measured in time and water. Consider a human lifetime of almost one hundred years—your grandparent and child seated on either end of your dinner table.

Rubber plantations, which cultivated rubber trees, scaled to a commercial level in 1902 and continue to be managed by farmers today. In Bangalore, Karnataka, where my grandfather was born in 1923, four British companies leased the land ten years prior from the British Raj for a term of 999 years. This is equivalent to the lifespan of thirty-three rubber trees, or forty generations of people.

In 1940, the term was reduced to ninety-nine years, and just before Partition in 1947—the fracture of land into Pakistan and India—the leases were deeded to local companies.

My grandfather translated Hindi to English in British classrooms before Partition. He was recast as an accountant in Pakistan.

Into English some words mutated more than others. Ossified were loot, jungle, pundit. Juggernaut from *Jagannath*, Lord of the Universe, became a mercilessly destructive force. Cushy, from *khushi*, happiness, became undemanding.

Logocentrism, the Western value preferencing the written or spoken word over that which it is referencing, is a strategy of conquest when it comes to translation. You replace one thing with another. To speak over another voice, fronting enough meaning. To write over existing text.

My grandfather passed away in 2003, nearly a decade before the British rubber tree plantation lease ended, nearly sixty years after paid translation. Though, after the proliferation of English in Pakistan, translation rooted itself between most teeth.

The first German reforestation plantation, founded in the late eighteenth century, had planned for production until 2050. You can log your memories until you grant the land ownership. You can rename it until it fits in your mouth. You can divide it according to property and afterlife until it sits trimmed in your palm.

You can pull up the roots and see where the trenches weave through the dirt. You can cover it in stone, gravel, under the uncaring line of the cartographer, but the earth remembers.

Rouse the match. The flame crawls to your fingers.

What can save you from burning? Only the body's electrical signal. Only the wind.

The controlled burning of the land, a traditional Indigenous stewardship practice, prevents capricious wildfires by diffusing seeds, by ingesting the weak underbrush and saplings. On Turtle Island, Indigenous knowledge has survived for over ten thousand years.

Fire disappears a house, a library, the people inside. Epistemicide: the destruction of a knowledge system. If you burn a book, you burn yourself endlessly, cauterize time itself.

Above an attentive blaze, seeds pour out of the hands of the pines, sequoia, and shrubs. Most of us are born with pokers in our palms, educated in the art of stoking.

Smoke gluts the air until we are barred from each other in boardrooms. It makes the breathing difficult, so we turn away, but it waits under our blue tent, slipping into our bedrooms.

I woke to the smoke once, believing the pain was originating from my body. Killed it with a pill then, like a stunned fly, nestled deeper into my sheets.

The crowning of a baby's skull is also called the ring of fire. The body remembers. Your hands, eyes, and tongue will speak for you when your mind fossilizes—petrified wood in a copper silence.

The most extreme form of protest is self-immolation. To divert the gaze of the public: games, circuses, gossip, mirrors. Pointing at the sky with a shriek.

The moon falling over the sun like a pupil. In place of birdsong: a cheering. The discussion of God, otherwise a godless eye, watching.

The first antagonist too was created by God. Instructed to pray during the eclipse, we stepped outside and stared instead, back at its unwavering gaze. Despite the warnings of seared retinas.

A sunset from the wrong direction is one of the most well-known signs of the end. For minutes, that cold glow appeared from every angle.

The name *Toronto* originates from the Mohawk word, *Tkaranto*, meaning "the place in the water where the trees stand." Wooden stakes arranged to catch fish, between the lips and the throat.

If a plot is a neighbourhood, a forest is a civilization. Consider proxy-wars, genocide, foreign-funded coups. Urbicide, the deliberate killing of a city and its infrastructure so the residents cannot return.

Architecture is a reflection of an era's prevalent social values. A memory planted for all to see, housing each decade to come. A shield from the snow and rain, the obliterating sun.

A witness, then a ghost with no tongue. Nearly trees, nearly water, their gazes passing over us into the landscape, flourishing quietly in the dark.

The trunks gain sight as they age, eyes hidden sometimes when over-whelmed. Thus, there are families that never see each other again. The soldier stole the girl's hands and she is still weeping, water slipping into her willowy hair.

In the childrens' book series, the word was passed through the trees that the lion-god had been killed on the stage of a stump.

The trees and the earth, under final law, will testify for or against us. The oaks, the teaks, the olive trees extend a branch only to be slashed off and placed as a centerpiece on the dinner table of your new home.

A popular game my elementary school classmates would play during the winter would take place in the planted tree clusters surrounding the playground. We would peel long white strips off of the paper birch trees and trade them for items, though I can't remember exactly what.

The game, as I understood it, was called "money," and I was too timid to ask about the pre-established rules.

Upon hearing the bell, we would hide our money under rocks, banked it under the snow, hoping it would not be thieved before we returned.

All season, I would join the others in skinning the trees, negotiating for items I didn't want. I remember my jealousy, not of the piles of skin tucked under their arms, but of their satisfaction.

Consequently, this was a game I always lost.

Research shows that an estimated one billion people from under-resourced and remote communities, or nearly a tenth of the human race, will die by 2100 if the post-industrial temperature rises by 2 degrees. The aim in 2015 was to reduce emissions, avoiding an increase from 0.98 to 1.5 degrees by 2045, but the rate has accelerated since.

In my safehouse, I am looking for a metaphor to convey this. I am not a storyteller—too prone to knotting the beginning to the end—but where there is a plot, I know there must be a narrator.

Let me cleave it apart instead.

Examining colonial history since 1850 and population growth, the cumulative CO_2 emitter ranking on a per-capita basis is, in this order, the Netherlands, the UK, Russia, the USA, and Canada. On this scale, India weighs in at about three percent of the UK.

Drain the water from the trees, the taps, the bodies. Drain the rain from the sky. From a higher moral ground, the archer lifts his bow and, for a moment, it takes the shape of a delicate ear.

In the last two decades, the logging industry, which is excluded from tracked emissions, has released more CO_2 than it has recaptured. The heat runs ten to one hundred times faster than the trees with their enviable rigidity can adapt.

Almost a quarter of the 1.5 degrees of heat was spent internationally on deforestation between 1850 and 1957, after which the impact of fossil fuels soared like ducks outside the queue for a dishwashing detergent bath.

On the graph, this activity appears to be *rising action*.

Of those famous five leaders in CO_2 emissions, two are net exporters, which means the emissions associated with exports are higher than those with imports. These goods are then frequently unloaded and unpackaged in the USA, Japan, and the UK.

Proclaimed the "workshop of the world" in the nineteenth century, Britain required primarily Indian resources to build railroads and ships to sustain their wars against France and Russia. Until recently, both France and Britain were connected by the political and economic privileges and duties accorded under the alliance known as the European Union.

Many countries today do not track emissions from their military and conflict-related activities. Many have declared that they will plant exactly one billion trees.

Some might say, given my history, I am not good with money, so I cannot possibly understand.

Under the weight of the sun's glare, I discover that we will arrive at 1.5 degrees by 2027.

What is it now, exactly, that we owe one another?

Peering into each other's browsing history, the CCTVs, the satellites. Perhaps this induces some particular fondness—ants in a glassed colony on the windowsill.

Foreign debt is what we owe.

Pakistan was to pay a $22.5 billion installment in 2023 after a third of the country, like Atlantis, was occupied by water. Nearly all of the fifty-four countries in the greatest need of debt relief are former colonies, a third of them formerly British-ruled, and over half will suffocate the quickest under the ballooning heat.

The ant farm holding half of the poorest people in the world—representing an unproductive three percent of the global economy—provides an optimal view for the owner. The ants make worlds of the soil, fashioning a life for themselves until you shake the box.

I plot the seeds over the graph and swear that they wriggle when I look away.

A report states that 1.2 billion people will be displaced by 2050 in the Global South, though "climate refugee" is still not a term recognized under international law. The lifeboat of the 1951 Refugee Convention would only protect those from violence and persecution directly caused by climate change, such as domestic conflicts over resources like water, as occurred in Chad, a former colony of France.

On television, the convention appears to be full of holes when "refugee" is traded for the "migrant," as if past profits did not leave lines of bread-crumbs in place of loaves.

Even a word will scorch your skin under glass, magnified through the window, under a painted blue canvas.

Birds were dropping dead from branches, from skies everywhere. India, the streets were cluttered with bats and monkeys. When a tree is dehydrated, it trembles in ultrasonic clicks. It cries.

Perspiration is an evolutionary strategy to cool the human body, but sweating is impossible when the heat is above wet-bulb temperature. After six hours, dysregulated organs will begin to fail. The first 2.2 billion victims of moist heatwaves will have lived in India and Pakistan, where the curtains have already been drawn.

One evening walk, I almost crushed a lime Tennessee warbler under my shoe. I wanted to memorialize it, thinking that this may never happen again.

Hogue: There is no scientific difference between a bomb dropped in a time of peace and in a time of war.

Peace manifests quite often as sedation, the numbing of a limb.

On Aristotle's stage, the actors in masks would sand our friction with society, with the outer world, before we returned to our daily lives. A representation of ourselves would satisfy our desires for more.

This is the role of the protagonist. Who doesn't love a yoked confession? A lullaby of validation.

Aber: We learn early on, especially in English, to use the active voice. It's inelegant to assume things happen to you; you do them. So the English *I* is active, capitalized. *I* has agency, so I must have agency.

English is the only language that capitalizes *I* in all scenarios. The Western canon has long since preferred free will over fate, which is the basis too for violations of the law. King-killer Macbeth shined his dagger until his reflection gleamed.

Theatre is reproduced all over the world, in and out of the colonies. Catastrophe is exorcized and final equilibrium attained for us so we all may slumber peacefully while the heat gnaws on our bones.

Years ago, I came upon a stump as wide as a stage.

My mother had warned me to keep my distance, lest the potential residents born of fire take an interest in me. So hot they blend into the wind, they reside in ancient trees and do whatever they please.

There is a photograph of me nearby, where I huddled into a hollow, where the innermost childhood rings once were.

Like an ax into flesh I stepped inside. I could have been possessed— something unnamable embedding itself between my ribs, lending a sharpness instead of breath.

A camera, a shovel, and a stake.

Yes, it has taken me so long I forgot I was searching for an answer.

Among the dead trunks, the tiny white sprouts rising from the forest floor finally deemed ghost pipes. Once used as a sedative, they survive by seizing nutrients from the tree roots.

The climate crisis has been called, by scientists, the sixth mass extinction.

Jordan: What shall we do, we who do not die, and we who did not burn?

In the forests of our jurisdiction, outside of them.

What rotted, what sat on the carcass, rubbed its hands again before feasting on whose flesh.

Cruelty is common, many-eyed, iridescent as water over oil.

The law follows you everywhere but the grave, where some of us settle, wearing our grandfathers' faces and the uniform of those who killed him.

History congeals inside the steel teapot, under our nail trimmings.

As we lay awake among beetles and maggots, our tails tucked under damp sheets lifted from the line.

We number the sheared stars, directing them toward us.

Maintaining peace with the unassuming cane, we too are called, and do we obey—

To be the lords of our own desperate little plots.

THE GARDEN

Still Life in the Garden

I am trying to make you laugh.
There: your favourite glass and pitcher,
a sheet on the grass. Blooms
I wish I could name, mountains alert
over the distant choir of insects.

Poking its head out from between my lips,
a word traces the angled light
from the curator's torch,
then tears at the crack in the paint.

New Year, New Me

The animal is always believed to begin, in the myths, at the navel.

There: the coarse fur, flaring scales, glistening
blubber, silken plumage, shell and horn and tooth.

Not hidden, but reserved,
the scientists note. *Reserved, but for what?*

asks the fish thrumming
in my chest. *How can I become*

more than what I am? I ask around
but the others shun us, since the fish
and I are naturally inclined to performing tricks
that end in governance.

How, I ask the scientists, *can I*
wrench her out?

We see it in war all the time: blood, cartilage, slicing
through the tail of the bone-beaded rope. I imagine

her eyes, swollen as eggs, in my throat.
The eyes I view for only moments in the mirror

each year when we unsheathe our heads.

In those dark rooms, water gathers around my face
and then waken those fabled slits.

Therefore, I have considered an insect-based diet,
discovering I'm not afraid of wings or a hundred
miniature legs. I propose an experiment

and cast the wide net of January. I know
if I'm buried as I am, from the dirt the insects would mine
my true hands, brow, heart.

One of these days, the conditions will be perfect.
Artificial light streaming down from above,
I will stopper my lungs.

Dip my hand into my saliva,

wait for a tug.

Hometown Elegy

Obsidian beetle falling to my knees—I tried to beat you
out of the bathroom rug and when I couldn't, I drowned you
in the washing machine. *Forgive me*, I murmured
to your body's accusation of my occupancy,
echoing through the wet steel tomb. What else

could I have said? It's true I know nothing of history—
Our history, corrects the bronzite insulation of crushed fishflies—
only the annual visits of the dirtied river travel further
inland to harass the parks and suffocate the gardens.
Only the celebrity thunderstorms passing through
the foreign crowds of industrial smog to urinate
through the neighbour's roof. Even the unseen doves
burn *Who? Who?* on my back after ten years of misnaming them.
On the indigo pavement, mangled earthworms
wriggle under the robins' incessant gossip, astonishing me.
Go home—they admonish through damp jade architecture
as they're carried away. I have lived here

long enough for a stranger to call it my hometown,
for its weather to discard my heart. I have poured
my face into its clean fresh water, meandered
along its river glittering with corporate light.
Through its afternoons' feverish conditioning, I kill
the ants in the kitchen and into my quick grey wrists
no epitaph is carved. I have killed

them each sensible summer, each romantic
spring. *Do you understand?*

the earth repeats, slower, enunciating
with its seismic tongue, *Are you listening?*
The deer hush, startled by my fidgeting. I watch
pristine grasses obediently swallow their stimulants.
Once, a raccoon let me hold its hand, but the dusty roses
veer away, their dried starlet curls still enduring
the city's pride. The witnessing sun laughs, *What good*

are you? as I knife the white curtains of wildflowers
only to lose them on my way home, my hands busied
in applause. The geese look me in the eye and shit
on every path, on every destination, on the poems
of another dreamy intruder marauding the view.

The View

My father is an excellent driver. Everyone knows so.
Half days stretched from coast to border,
then back. Through downtown, pedestrians
skittering like pigeons from the pavement.
Up the narrow roads carved into the western mountains—
quick as a devout breeze—as we pressed our faces
against the door and an unbelievable view.

On my way home between the pastoral slopes,
I find I can see it all—the morning fields mumbling
under fresh light, the barn roofs crushed like rotten tomatoes,
haze of cows drifting, like hours, up to the fence—

only now, in my periphery. So long
a passenger, my novel eager that my gaze
return from the window—the solid frame
in which futures appeared as glutted
as each bright crop nodding
above the gloved hands of my dreams.

Mouth ajar, all this time I would sleep
and wake to more beauty, nameless or known,
my father's eyes fixed on the searing sun.

The Pear

I've been thinking about this pear all morning and afternoon.
Stopped in the middle of cleaning the washroom, bleach
still on my palms, to sit down and tell you
about this green-gold fortune, its hundred tiny winks.
That moment of relief from the daily apple,
hard and unyielding as a stirred coal. I close my eyes
and envy K, who would eat both the core and the wooden stem.
I envied too the light that cooed over the pear
as a seed, the branch that rocked it sweetly
as it swelled with inarticulable desire.
And later, the bird with first access
to its ten hearts, the grassy bed that cradled it
far from the disagreements of the seasons.
The pear fostered by hand after hand, miracle
after miracle, before arriving here, exerted
from all this becoming. It petals open,
honest and good at a gentle blade.

One day, when we return to the earth,
and our souls are elsewhere
I'll remember my admission—
that, against the oncoming evening,
I still loved the world.

Larvae

Out of the blue, honey from the yellow
mothering of pleated daisies, velveteen roses, buttons
of butterfly bush. Heads stuffed with sweetness,
I imagine a meal with her,
she who worries about my infested cheeks,
my arid stalks of hair.

If nectar is as nourishing as they say, I will
not touch it. From across the green spread,
I know the bitterness of pollen—as a child, I licked
its dust from my palm and petaled out my tongue.

Who, with such heavy feet,
would carry home this floral blood?
Knead into it some worth?

I had flicked the bright young heads
of dandelions into the wind, rubbed their faces
on my fists to form two bossy suns.
Four hundred miles away,

her fingers are just above the cobalt-gold ring
of the stove, flipping discs of dough. She texts me
smoothie recipes for my skin, egg masks for my hair
until it glimmers like a crown. One day, I will see her
for the last time through a screen, through a door—

One of us on the inside of the black net,
the other beating her small hands against it.

Heaven

Before the white peaks and idyllic valleys,
my mother said, *If you think this is beautiful,*

just imagine how heaven will be.
The distance of a thought, of time.

I could never elude the gaze
of the mountains, even years later.

At their feet, on the maintained trails
we had heard panting, as heavy to the ear

as a pulse. In dissuasion, we called on the bright tones
of nostalgia, directed our laughter toward the deciduous.

Playing dead is the recommended course
of action, while evasion wakes desire,

but only if confronted.
We were, at that moment, alone

and afraid. Not of our footprints of course,
but of the light that would exhume them.

The Firefly May or May Not Carry Poison

Inside its heavy hull a jewel fatal
or false, one of dozens floating by the fence.
Untethering from the eager climbing leaves,
they sway toward me. Who, now,

is the eyed tower and who the blossom?
Drifting so close I could swallow them,
they project a golden seed onto my cheek.
Indifferent, as if there is such a thing as light

that does not kill. I had held them in damp
hands, gazed for hours from behind glass.
Who could resist? And so, I was not good

at making friends. A child must burn
before they fear flame, the theory of smoke.
Must be warned not to touch what is costly—
what, in another life, could power a world.

Now that I have grown, I have learned
to cut away at my imagination during the day,
to shine it with the shadows into a cosmic dream.

In less than a month, the fireflies will die
while I, the hot summer stone, will still be
here in the yard, kneeling.

Departure for Noah's Ark

Hold my rusted pond-mirror and follow me
down this buttercup-swathed path to somewhere safe.
Block the skyline's shallow praise from
over everything I've ever killed, from the cold star
I fused to the gate outside my heart.
Forget the blaring premiere of another day
wasted, the tinselled actors fleeing
from the show and the audiences of wind
broken into countries: we're running late.
Maybe next time we'll see the end of this, but for now
help me lift the butterflies' wealth of irises, their hydrangea
mines, some slackened rainbows of roses, and these final
seasons of tragedy.

Remember how we abandoned the weather
to the machines—their hollering relentless
as dogs—and left it concussed
for the children? You can still see it
over there, over the burning hill
of industry, where we expect the clashes
of rain, of flame, of stone. Even here,
we stumble over limbs, outstretched fingers,
our mouths wing-netted, pupils blossomed
blank. Don't worry, I've already released
the laboured bees from each map,
and packed the colors I cannot see   in case

the flood   in case the ice   the blushing rock
striking the land   the musical interlude.

Whatever you do, don't invite the credits
on this disaster film, only the attendance tracked
and printed in the sky, in the poem
holding a last gasp inside my lungs.

Pay attention. I'm tired

of preparing obituaries. Lost my voice
to the vacuums of money, buried its soundless
casket and can now only mimic the prayers
of the light's cool laughter, its dewy face
pressed against the earth. I pray for us

in the chronic daydreams between sharp-footed lightning
and its shadowed trumpets, behind the trees
in their twisting skirts of precipitation, spoiled
gardenia tulle and flocks of emerald ruffle.
I admit, hidden under my spine is the topaz
hope of a wet streetlamp. So you—
yes, you—your armies of dandelion lit like space,
whose fluttering seeds clog my brain a rubbery grey
may climb into my pockets. Hurry up
before I change my mind. As for the unsoiled air,

please cauterize our throats like dawn.

Waters untouched by metal,
I ask you to let us drink one last time
while I search for our names in the mythic constellations
of wrongful murder—for any monument
of our bodies—and locate not so much as a needle
of enlightenment. I watch the moon, in my periphery,

watch me. Rude, isn't it? What good is a witness
who can't testify? Who doesn't caution?
It was never on our side of course, but who
could blame it? Every night waves the flat black flag
of a window for an animal infant unmet
by its mother's sound. Through the dusk
doorway, the tired azure of the sky's gaze
points away from us. Forgiveness,

hold the door. We're coming,
even as the same summer darkens a shade
each year from thirst, even as the cruel winter carries its water
elusive and volatile. We're coming
even if this morning parallels all others
because I promised this yawning century
tickets to a new world. Changed out of a dress
mourned white, banished futures spent
in the foreign planets of my head. Take my passport

while I slip memory into my hair—you'll never find it—
and enter the procession of everything

I'm afraid of, behind the beasts that could play fetch
with our skulls: How I've loved to look
at them, and look up I do

to our routine extinction wielding the rubied sword
of the horizon. It blinks a single eye
and the hand-carved tide nears

but the boat is here,
mast open to every worthy breath.

Nausicaä of the Valley of the Wind

Driving south to my parents' house for the holidays
between fields of soybean, corn, and wheat
now cut close to the earth and dried in the November sun.
The two highway lanes are encroached by darkness
despite the rain, construction, and our predestined speed.

On the screen, the beetles guard the blue trees
not yet known to purify our last hope for soil and water.
Green and mountainous, they chase trespassers into the desert
then wait in the shadows split by their bloody glare.

Beyond my headlights, a forest of windmills is invisible
until they blink all at once—flashing rubies
halfway up the sky, three arms waving on and on—
beside power structures buzzing in shiny alien lattices.

Nausicaä opens her hands to the insects and they swaddle her
in memory. Through the warm lens of the past: a child,
six-legged and hidden in a tree, from a king with the best of intentions.

It's not that late but still the hours pin my skin down to the bone.
At this velocity, a mistake would be fatal, so I say aloud,
perhaps to myself, perhaps to anyone listening,
Don't worry, we will make it there.
We'll make it home.

The Endangered Monarch Butterfly
Lives for Seven Months or Six Weeks

I had supplicated, and thus I am received
into an afternoon of reading—unbound by the fences
of anxiety, a clear balm stroking my nape.

Yet my gaze clings to the handsome ginger
hanging from the violet snout of a summer lilac
until satiated, coaxed into the sweating kingdoms
of onyx-pedalling susans, tusked jasmine, and silk-tuned roses,
from where he is guided through the volatile troop
of grasses by the grace of our shared zephyr,
back to those rapturous wrists to lounge.
Glistening as elegantly as a copper watch,
as if to say, *Of course*
                    you can enjoy your life.

So struck am I
I forget my fantasy in my hands.

Self Portrait with Polar Bear

I.

On BBC Earth, a polar bear reaches across the soundless arena
to tear at another's neck with a wet, black maw, a paw
crushing its head with a shadowy grip. They then alternate,
faces blued in Arctic light, and stand nearly ten feet in height
between a shattered window of land and the stone sky.

It's late autumn, but they are in their fresh summer dresses,
hungry as stars. Masked with blood, they chase me up
the boardwalk fencing in my dreams, swipe at my ankles
until I'm more hours than meat.

They leave, then, still seasonal friends
searching for lunch.

II.

I don't dream about the zoo in Oklahoma, where a bear
soaked in old seal oil gazes beyond the photographer.
Spit foaming around a rot-purple tongue and sulphurous teeth,
I recoil from his image, heart throbbing like cold water.

Never mind that he's dead as the picture—
that another May, his kidney surrendered
under a pelt sour as milk.

Never mind that he belongs
to no one, not even to the city where he sleeps.
His name drifts like fog under the morning heat.

III.

How sick I am with beauty,

how spoiled of light.

Mercy

My first time fishing, I flung the seizure
back into the water after my terrible thread
and needle wove through its silver cheek.
I knew I would become a murderer
the moment I hesitated, stunned by the aim
of its serrated glimmer. Stranger,

I should have split you jaw to iridescent junction,
reaped mercy. Were you too a child,
your current parallel to mine?
Or were you on your way home, finally,
after years of enduring the cold alone?

Minute hand dammed, that hour's echo
ripples between my ears and you, baffled, appeal
to my ankles each time I slip into the cool silk
of the lake. And when I return at the end
of another unremarkable evening,

out of the kitchen sink your bright eyes cut—
a body made of two heavy halves.

Oryx

Manufactured behind its onyx and pearl windows,
it's the oryx's cool-headedness I envy. I have only two
brutish stones fountaining from my skull—

one from my private mind, the other blunted
in clarifying opposition. Gladiating

when I was disappeared by the steel of the world,
it was by its guilted echo, then,
that I was fortunate to have been returned,

though cultivated as a shadow.
I masticate one of my bones,
harvesting its centre with a dull blade

while the sun captures another arid field each year.
It excavates a similar room in my chest

where, always, there is a smaller animal
with a glittering mirror
for a face.

Born to brace a pendulous neck under rotating hands,
to pound this interior with its four heavy spades.

Beyond the wall, someone is tearing an arrow

from leather, nocking it behind their mouth.

I follow suit, removing a single pointed horn
to sheath in my throat

and receive, finally, an answer
without the desperate sound.

Here, Grass

Dead, we will be perfect.
Burying evolution with our two bodies—
here are the last northern white rhinoceroses, and then,
nothing. Don't worry. After 55 million years,
the body will hit us like a season. The grass
will be freshly dewed, the grass will be parched
blond, but the grass will rise.
It depends on the intimacy of the hand—
how the bruise will hush
when you see it coming, like a rain
of vultures crushing the plot.
But dig long enough, and the soft blades
will meet your square mouth, your swollen throat.
When mine contracted, I lay there,
motionless, waiting for an end.
Panic is just a gust that intends to stop
in the body, but flushes through to the other side.
Panic is the grass of self-preservation
so naturally, we never want nightfall, to be consumed
by the unfamiliar morning. I live
until the dark knocks and my body
collapses toward the inevitable,
the routine. By the daily shadow of the public
we will be held until our memory dissolves,
so don't be afraid. After us, nothing will change.
The horn will meet the skull, the calloused flesh,

the bones. The stone hoof will meet the grass, wherever it may be, and we will be together.

Notes and Bibliography

The definition of "Shadow Price" is sourced from *Collins Dictionary*.

Shadow Price
"The median estimate of a statistical value of a life is about $4.9 million" is from Michele Campolieti's notes from the Economics of Healthcare course taught at the University of Toronto.

TIME
The epigraph "I have seen your true face: the back of your head" is from Richard Siken's poem "Birds Hover the Trampled Field" from *War of the Foxes*.

The Dream-Eaters
The poem uses Andri Snær Magnason's concept of breaking down the climate crisis into time and water. He uses lifespans to quantify long durations of time and, in one example, places his grandmother and child at the same table, representing two hundred years across the past and future.

The epigraph is from "Birds Falling out of the Sky in Mass Die-Off in South-Western US" by Phoebe Weston.

The phrase "nearby is the country they call life" is from Rainer Maria Rilke's poem "Go to the Limits of Your Longing."

Natural History Museum
The ending of this poem is inspired by Franny Choi's "Catastrophe Is Next to Godliness."

The Whale
The epigraph is a quote from Ursula K. Le Guin's speech at the 2014 National Book Awards.

The background on the human lifespan is from "Humans Could Live up to 150 Years, New Research Suggests" by Emily Willingham.

The information on the carbon conversion of whales is from "A Strategy to Protect Whales Can Limit Greenhouse Gases and Global Warming" by Ralph Chami, Thomas Cosimano, Connel Fullenkamp, and Sena Oztosun.

Birthday Poem
The term "climate change denial" was first used in the year 2000, according to the *Merriam-Webster Dictionary*.

THE LAST POET IN THE WORLD
This section is indebted to Solmaz Sharif's work on the role of the poet, especially in her poem "Patronage."

The epigraph "Very early in my life it was too late" is from *The Lover* by Marguerite Duras.

Maybe I should've been a stenographer
The premise takes inspiration from Diane Seuss's poem "I should have been in cinema. I should have been in paint" in *frank: sonnets.*

THE PLOT

This section would not exist without the essay "Notes on Craft: Writing in the Hour of Genocide" by Fargo Naissim Tbakhi, particularly the ideas on witness, catharthis, and the power of poetry and language.

"A tool in a certain hand is renamed a weapon" is indebted to Richard Siken's line "The hand sings weapon. The mind says tool." in the poem "Landscape with Blur of Conquerors."

The information on pests and pesticides is sourced from "Denser Forests Across the USA Experience More Damage from Insects and Pathogens" by Christopher Asaro, Frank H. Koch, and Kevin M. Potter; "UMass Extension Landscape," Nursery and Urban Forestry Program of the University of Massachusetts Amherst; "Limiting the Impact of Insect Pests on Urban Trees Under Climate Change" by Samiya Tabassum and Anthony Manea; "Urban Tree Isolation Affects the Abundance of Its Pests and Their Natural Enemies" by André Garcia, Pedro Gonçalves Vaz, José Carlos Franco, Pedro Nunes, Hervé Jactel, Manuela Branco; *Forest Microbiology: Tree Diseases and Pests* by Kai Wang, Iiro Miettinen, Emad H. Jaber, and Fred O. Asiegbu; "Microbial Symbionts of Herbivorous Species Across the Insect Tree" by Enric Frago, Sharon E. Zytynska, and Nina E. Fatouros in *Advances in Insect Physiology Vol. 58*; Dr. Nadina Galle's doctoral research, "The Internet of Nature"; and "Environmental and Health Effects of Pesticide Residues" by Sajjad Ali, Muhammad Irfan Ullah, Asif Sajjad, Qaiser Shakeel, and Azhar Hussain.

Cloud seeding is a weather modification technique that induces rain, and has been used historically to infuse rainwater with silver iodide for military operations.

The history of European and Indian forest management is sourced from "Deep Roots: A Conceptual History of 'Sustainable Development' (Nachhaltigkeit)" by Ulrich Grober; "State Forestry and Social Conflict in British India: A Study in the Ecological Basis of Agrarian Protest" by Ramachandra Guha and Madhav Gadgil; "The Forest Act of 1878," the Indian Ministry of Culture; "Contesting the Resource: The Politics of Forest Management in Colonial Burma" by Raymond Leslie Bryant; "The Origins of Timber Plantations in India" by Brett M. Bennett; "Sustainable Forestry Science: Wilhelm Philip Daniel Schlich," the Biodiversity Heritage Library; "Sustainable Forest Management— A Principle Developed in Central Europe," the Sommerauer Forest Sector Advisory Services; "Evolution of Silviculture Thinning: Rejection to Transcendence" by Boris Zeide; "Pre-Colonial and Colonial Forest Culture in the Presidency of Bengal" by Somnath Ghosal; "The British Art of Colonialism in India: Subjugation and Division" by Aziz Rahman, Mohsin Ali, and Saad Kahn; and "Teak Conquest. Wars, Forest Imperialism and Shipbuilding in India (1793–1815)" by Lucas Sérougne.

The history of rubber plantations in India are sourced from "From Plantations to Reserve Forests" by Anil Kumar M and "Growth of Rubber Plantation in India—An Overview" by Sukanta Sarkar.

The stanza on logocentrism uses information from "Betraying Empire: Translation and the Ideology of Conquest" by Vicente L. Rafael.

The information on current forest management and agriculture is sourced from "Managed to Death: How Canada Turned Its Forests into a Carbon Bomb" by Barry Saxifrage; "Environmental Impacts of Glyphosate in Ontario's Forestry Industry" by Olyvia Foster; "The Constraints of

Selecting for Insect Resistance in Plantation Trees" by Martin L Henery; and "Plant Defense Against Herbivorous Pests: Exploiting Resistance and Tolerance Traits for Sustainable Crop Protection" by Carolyn Mitchell, Rex M. Brennan, Julie Graham, and Alison J. Karley.

The information on climate debt susceptibility and colonial emissions is sourced from "Avoiding 'Too Little Too Late' on International Debt Relief" by Lars Jensen; "Revealed: How Colonial Rule Radically Shifts Historical Responsibility for Climate Change" by Simon Evans and Verner Viisainen; "Analysis: Which Countries Are Historically Responsible for Climate Change?" by Simon Evans; the Global Carbon Project's fossil CO_2 emissions dataset by Robbie M. Andrew and Glen P. Peters; "How Do CO_2 Emissions Compare When We Adjust for Trade?" by Hannah Ritchie; "Decoding Modern Colonialism: The Sovereign Debt Quagmire in the Global South" by Rameen Siddiqui; and the Debt Relief for Green and Inclusive Recovery (DRGR) project report: *Defaulting on Development and Climate—Debt Sustainability and the Race for the 2030 Agenda and Paris Agreement.*

The information on the progression and future of climate change is sourced from "Greatly Enhanced Risk to Humans as a Consequence of Empirically Determined Lower Moist Heat Stress Tolerance" by Daniel J. Vecellio, Qinqin Kong, W. Larry Kenney, and Matthew Huber; "Quantifying Global Greenhouse Gas Emissions in Human Deaths to Guide Energy Policy" by Joshua M. Pearce and Richard Parncutt; the Institute for Economics and Peace's Global Peace Index 2024 report and Ecological Threat Report 2023; "Climate Change and Displacement: The Myths and the Facts" by Kristy Siegfried; and "Temperature Is Likely to

Exceed 1.5°C Above Pre-Industrial Level Temporarily in Next 5 Years" by the World Meteorological Organization.

"There is no scientific difference between a bomb dropped in a time of peace and in a time of war" is a quote by Dr. Rebecca Hogue from her "'Anneal this Breath': Reading Glass, Poetics, and Nuclear Genealogies with Yhonnie Scarce in South Australia" seminar.

The information on Aristotle's theatre is sourced from August Boal's *Theatre of the Oppressed* and Fargo Naissim Tbakhi's interpretations in "Notes on Craft: Writing in the Hour of Genocide."

"We learn early on, especially in English, to use the active voice ..." is from the poem "Rilke and I" from *Hard Damage* by Aria Aber.

"What shall we do, we who do not die ..." is a modified phrase from June Jordan's keynote presentation at Barnard College.

THE GARDEN
The Pear
The premise of this poem is indebted to "The Orange" by Wendy Cope.

Departure for Noah's Ark
The premise is inspired by Shira Erlichman's poem "Somewhere Real."

Oryx
The beginning of this poem is inspired by Aria Aber's poem, "Self-Portrait as the Wounded Doe of Artemis."

Here, Grass
This poem modifies the phrase "hit the body like a season" from Ocean Vuong's poem "A Little Closer to the Edge."

Acknowledgements

I'm grateful to the editors of the following publications, in which earlier versions or excerpts of these poems appeared:

AHVAZ // AAVAZ // AVAAZ: A Chapbook Anthology of South Asian Poetry: "Oryx"
Augur: "Departure for Noah's Ark"
Canthius: "Birthday Poem"
CBC Books: "The Pear"
Hart House Review: "Self Portrait with Polar Bear"
Poetry Pause: "Here, Grass"
The Seventh Wave: "The Jungle Book: Epilogue"
The Walrus: "Mercy"

*

I'd like to thank first and foremost my dear family, especially my sister, for carving a path for me to follow my dreams. Thank you for always believing in me, even when I don't believe in myself. I'm grateful too for my wonderful friends and their relentless encouragement. Thank you all for your love and patience.

Thank you to Rachana Hegde, my first reader, for your expansive friendship and careful attention. Meeting you was the highlight of my teenage writing years and I'd glad you've been with me for every step of this journey.

I'm grateful to the following poets who, through their work, taught me how to write poetry, and continue to show me the limitlessness of the genre: Solmaz Sharif, Aria Aber, Richard Siken, Daniel Borzutsky, Safia Elhillo, Fatimah Asghar, Natalie Diaz, Sanna Wani, Natalie Wee, Yasmin Belkhyr, Jess Rizkallah, Ocean Vuong, and K-Ming Chang. Thank you for inspiring me each time I sit down at my desk to write.

Thank you to all of the teachers, editors, and strangers who have had kind words to say about my writing, particularly when I started developing my craft.

Thank you to Kevin and the rest of the House of Anansi team for your support as we turned this manuscript into a book. Additionally, I'm grateful to the Ontario Arts Council for its support.

Thank you to everyone who is making the future a place we can all thrive in. You make me more optimistic than ever before, and I know that we can create a sustainable world together.

And, as always, I'm most grateful to the Most Gracious, the Most Merciful.

FARAH GHAFOOR is an award-winning poet living on the traditional territory of the Anishnabeg, the Mississaugas of the Credit, the Chippewa, the Haudenosaunee, and the Wendat Peoples. Her work was awarded the E.J. Pratt Medal and Prize in Poetry, longlisted for the CBC Poetry Prize, is taught in university courses, and published in *The Walrus*, *The Fiddlehead*, *Room*, and elsewhere. Raised in New Brunswick and southern Ontario, Ghafoor now works in Tkaronto (Toronto) as an accountant.